RESPIRATORY CARE IN SURGERY

TABLE OF CONTENT

INTRODUCTION 2
MODULE ONE 3
    LESSON ONE: Understanding Respiratory Physiology 3
    LESSON TWO: PREOPERATIVE RESPIRATORY ASSESSMENT AND PREPARATION 5
MODULE TWO...10
    LESSON ONE: Intraoperative Respiratory Management 10
    LESSON TWO: Postoperative Respiratory Care and Monitoring.. 14
MODULE THREE..19
    LESSON ONE: COMMON RESPIRATORY COMPLICATIONS IN SURGERY AND THEIR MANAGEMENT.........................19
    LESSON TWO: Respiratory Therapies and Interventions in Surgical Patients..23
MODULE FOUR 29
    LESSON ONE: The Role of Multidisciplinary Teams in Respiratory Care..29
    LESSON TWO: Future Trends in Respiratory Care....................33
MODULE FIVE 37
    LESSON ONE: Ethical Considerations in Respiratory Care.......37
MODULE SIX 41
    LESSON ONE: Cultural Competence in Respiratory Care.........41
MODULE SEVEN..45
    LESSON ONE: Psychological Aspects of Respiratory Care.......45
CONCLUSION 48
REFERENCES...49

COURSE OVERVIEW

This course is designed to provide healthcare providers with an in-depth understanding of respiratory care in the context of surgery. Covering preoperative assessments, intraoperative management, postoperative care, and advanced respiratory support techniques, this course equips participants with the knowledge and skills necessary to optimize patient outcomes. The curriculum also addresses ethical considerations, cultural competence, psychological aspects, and future trends in respiratory care. Through a combination of theoretical knowledge and practical applications, participants will learn to deliver high-quality respiratory care across the surgical continuum.

COURSE OBJECTIVE

By the end of this course, participants will be able to Understand the Fundamentals of Respiratory Care in Surgery, Conduct Comprehensive Preoperative Respiratory Assessments, Implement Effective Intraoperative Respiratory Management, Optimize Postoperative Respiratory Care, Utilize Advanced Respiratory Therapies and Interventions and, Foster Multidisciplinary Collaboration. This course aims to enhance the expertise of healthcare providers in respiratory care within the surgical context, ensuring improved patient outcomes and professional growth in this critical area of healthcare.

COURSE MATERIALS

To learn this course, **healthcare providers/ participants** must be provided with materials like a Pen, pencil, notebook, and notepad to better understand and make it easy for them to learn.

INTRODUCTION

In the dynamic and often complex environment of surgical care, respiratory management stands as a critical pillar supporting patient outcomes. The respiratory system's integral role in maintaining homeostasis means that any perturbation, whether preoperative, intraoperative, or postoperative, can significantly impact a patient's recovery and overall prognosis. Therefore, mastering the nuances of respiratory care in surgery is essential for healthcare providers who aim to deliver the highest standards of care.

This book, "Mastering Respiratory Care in Surgery: A Comprehensive Guide for Healthcare Providers," is designed to equip medical professionals with the knowledge and skills necessary to manage respiratory care effectively throughout the surgical process. Whether you are a seasoned practitioner or a newcomer to the field, this guide offers valuable insights and practical advice that will enhance your competence and confidence in managing surgical patients.

MODULE ONE

LESSON ONE: UNDERSTANDING RESPIRATORY PHYSIOLOGY

Respiratory physiology is the foundation upon which effective respiratory care is built. Understanding how the respiratory system functions 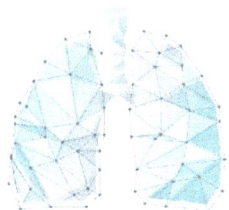 under normal conditions and how it responds to the stress of surgery is crucial for healthcare providers. The primary function of the respiratory system is to facilitate gas exchange, ensuring oxygen is delivered to the bloodstream and carbon dioxide is expelled from the body. This process involves the coordinated effort of the lungs, airways, diaphragm, and accessory muscles, all regulated by neural and chemical controls.

The Impact of Surgery on the Respiratory System

Surgery, particularly major operations, can significantly impact the respiratory system. The stress response to surgery includes the release of catecholamines and other stress hormones, which can lead to increased oxygen consumption and carbon dioxide production. Additionally, general anesthesia and mechanical ventilation can alter normal respiratory mechanics and gas exchange, potentially leading to hypoxemia and hypercapnia if not properly managed.

Preoperative Considerations

Effective respiratory care begins long before the patient enters the operating room. A thorough preoperative respiratory assessment is essential to identify any preexisting conditions that might affect respiratory function during and after surgery. This assessment includes a detailed patient history, physical examination, and appropriate diagnostic tests such as spirometry, arterial blood gas analysis, and chest imaging.

Patients with chronic respiratory conditions such as chronic obstructive pulmonary disease (COPD), asthma, or restrictive lung disease require special attention. Optimization of their respiratory status through bronchodilators, corticosteroids, and other therapies can reduce the risk of perioperative complications. Smoking cessation, ideally initiated weeks before surgery, is another crucial step in preoperative respiratory care.

Intraoperative Management

During surgery, maintaining adequate oxygenation and ventilation is paramount. Anesthesiologists play a critical role in monitoring respiratory parameters and adjusting ventilation settings to match the patient's needs. This includes selecting the appropriate mode of ventilation, adjusting tidal volumes, and ensuring positive end-expiratory pressure (PEEP) to prevent atelectasis.

Monitoring techniques such as capnography, pulse oximetry, and arterial blood gas analysis are essential tools that provide real-time feedback on the patient's respiratory status. Anesthesiologists must also be vigilant for signs of respiratory complications such as bronchospasm, aspiration, and pneumothorax, which require prompt intervention.

Postoperative Respiratory Care

The postoperative period is a vulnerable time for respiratory complications. Patients emerging from anesthesia may experience residual effects that depress respiratory drive, leading to hypoventilation. Pain, particularly from thoracic or upper abdominal surgeries, can also inhibit effective coughing and deep breathing, increasing the risk of atelectasis and pneumonia.

Postoperative respiratory care focuses on monitoring and supporting adequate ventilation and oxygenation. Techniques such as incentive spirometry, chest physiotherapy, and early mobilization are employed to promote lung expansion and prevent complications. Pain management, including the use of epidural analgesia or regional blocks, can facilitate better respiratory function by allowing patients to breathe and cough more effectively.

DISCUSSION QUESTIONS

- How do different surgical procedures influence the type and intensity of respiratory care required postoperatively?
- What are the key physiological changes in the respiratory system during surgery, and how can healthcare providers mitigate their impacts?

LESSON TWO: PREOPERATIVE RESPIRATORY ASSESSMENT AND PREPARATION

Preoperative Pulmonary Risk Evaluation

RISKS
1. Patient-related — Pulmonary, Nonpulmonary
2. Surgery-related
3. Anesthesia-related

EVALUATION
- IN ALL PATIENTS: Medical history, Physical exam
- IN SELECTED PATIENTS: Blood tests, Chest x-ray, Pulmonary function test, RISK STRATIFICATIONS

The preoperative assessment is a critical step in surgical planning, particularly for respiratory care. This phase allows healthcare providers to identify and address any existing respiratory issues that could complicate surgery and recovery. A thorough preoperative assessment provides a baseline against which postoperative changes can be measured and guides interventions to optimize respiratory function before the patient undergoes surgery.

Patient History and Physical Examination

A comprehensive patient history is the cornerstone of the preoperative respiratory assessment. Key components include:

- **Smoking History:** Document the patient's smoking status, including pack-years and the duration of smoking cessation if applicable. Smoking is a significant risk factor for respiratory complications, and smoking cessation interventions should be initiated as early as possible.
- **Previous Surgeries and Anesthesia:** Review the patient's surgical history and any previous complications related to anesthesia or respiratory issues. This information can help anticipate and mitigate risks during the upcoming procedure.
- **Chronic Respiratory Conditions:** Identify any existing respiratory conditions such as COPD, asthma, interstitial lung disease, or sleep apnea. Understanding the severity and current management of these conditions is essential for planning perioperative care.
- **Medications and Allergies:** Document all current medications, particularly those that affect respiratory function, such as bronchodilators, corticosteroids, and immunosuppressants. Additionally, note any known drug allergies or adverse reactions.

The physical examination should focus on respiratory signs and symptoms, including breath sounds, respiratory rate, and effort. Look for signs of respiratory distress, cyanosis, or clubbing of the fingers, which may indicate chronic hypoxemia.

Diagnostic Tests

Several diagnostic tests are used to assess respiratory function preoperatively:

- **Spirometry**: Measures lung volumes and flow rates, providing information about obstructive or restrictive lung

disease. Key parameters include forced vital capacity (FVC) and forced expiratory volume in one second (FEV1).
- **Arterial Blood Gas (ABG) Analysis:** Assesses gas exchange by measuring oxygen and carbon dioxide levels in the blood. ABG analysis can identify hypoxemia, hypercapnia, and acid-base imbalances.
- **Chest Imaging:** Chest X-rays or computed tomography (CT) scans can reveal structural abnormalities, infections, or other conditions that might impact respiratory function.
- **Pulse Oximetry:** Provides a non-invasive measure of oxygen saturation, which is useful for ongoing monitoring.

Optimization of Respiratory Status

Once potential respiratory issues are identified, steps should be taken to optimize the patient's respiratory status before surgery:

- **Smoking Cessation:** Encourage and support smoking cessation. Even short-term cessation can improve respiratory function and reduce the risk of complications.
- **Bronchodilator Therapy:** For patients with obstructive lung disease, optimize bronchodilator therapy to improve airway patency.
- **Steroid Therapy:** Patients with asthma or COPD may benefit from corticosteroid therapy to reduce airway inflammation.
- **Vaccinations:** Ensure that patients are up to date on vaccinations, including influenza and pneumococcal vaccines, to reduce the risk of respiratory infections.

Preoperative Education

Educating patients about the importance of respiratory care and the role they play in optimizing their outcomes is a crucial component of preoperative preparation. Key topics to cover include:

- **Breathing Exercises:** Teach patients diaphragmatic breathing and incentive spirometry exercises to practice before surgery.

These exercises can help maintain lung capacity and prevent postoperative complications.
- **Pain Management:** Explain how effective pain management can facilitate better respiratory function by allowing patients to take deep breaths and cough effectively.
- **Postoperative Expectations:** Discuss what patients can expect after surgery, including the use of oxygen therapy, respiratory monitoring, and the importance of early mobilization.

Preoperative Fasting and Medication Instructions

Provide clear instructions regarding preoperative fasting and medication management:

- **Fasting Guidelines:** Follow standard fasting guidelines to reduce the risk of aspiration during induction of anesthesia.
- **Medication Adjustments:** Instruct patients on which medications to continue and which to withhold before surgery. For example, continue essential medications like bronchodilators but withhold medications that might increase bleeding risk.

Special Considerations for High-Risk Patients

Patients with significant respiratory comorbidities or those undergoing high-risk surgeries require additional considerations:

- **Preoperative Pulmonary Rehabilitation:** For patients with severe chronic respiratory conditions, a structured pulmonary rehabilitation program can improve overall fitness and respiratory function.
- **Consultation with Specialists:** Involve pulmonologists, anesthesiologists, and other specialists in the preoperative planning for high-risk patients.
- **Advanced Planning for Postoperative Care:** Develop a detailed postoperative care plan, including potential ICU

admission and the use of advanced respiratory support techniques if needed.

The preoperative respiratory assessment and preparation phase is a vital step in ensuring optimal outcomes for surgical patients. By thoroughly assessing respiratory function, identifying and addressing any existing issues, and educating patients on their role in respiratory care, healthcare providers can significantly reduce the risk of complications and enhance recovery. The next lesson will focus on intraoperative respiratory management, detailing the techniques and strategies used to maintain respiratory stability during surgery.

DISCUSSION QUESTIONS

- Why is a comprehensive preoperative respiratory assessment crucial for surgical patients, and what are the potential consequences of neglecting this step?
- How can preoperative interventions improve postoperative respiratory outcomes, and what specific strategies should be implemented?

MODULE TWO

LESSON ONE: INTRAOPERATIVE RESPIRATORY MANAGEMENT

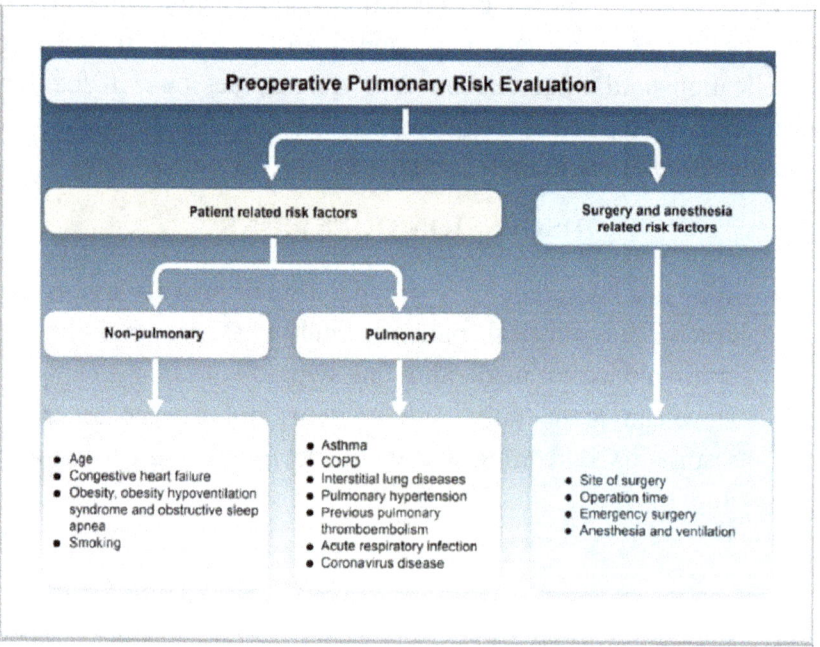

Intraoperative respiratory management is critical to ensuring patient safety and optimal outcomes during surgery. Anesthesia and surgical procedures can significantly impact respiratory function, necessitating careful monitoring and intervention to maintain adequate oxygenation and ventilation. This lesson provides an in-depth exploration of the principles and practices involved in intraoperative respiratory care.

Anesthetic Considerations

The choice of anesthetic technique can greatly influence respiratory management. General anesthesia, in particular, requires a detailed understanding of its effects on the respiratory system:

- **Effects of Anesthetics on Respiration:** General anesthetics depress central respiratory drive, reduce tidal volumes, and alter ventilation-perfusion matching. These effects necessitate close monitoring and adjustment of ventilation settings.
- **Airway Management:** Secure airway management is paramount. Techniques include endotracheal intubation, laryngeal mask airway (LMA) placement, and, in some cases, awake fiberoptic intubation for patients with difficult airways.

Mechanical Ventilation Strategies

Mechanical ventilation is a cornerstone of intraoperative respiratory management. Key aspects include:

- **Ventilation Modes:** Common modes include volume-controlled ventilation (VCV) and pressure-controlled ventilation (PCV). The choice of mode depends on patient-specific factors and surgical requirements.
- **Tidal Volume and Respiratory Rate:** Set tidal volumes typically at 6-8 mL/kg of predicted body weight to minimize the risk of ventilator-induced lung injury. Adjust the respiratory rate to maintain adequate minute ventilation and normocapnia.
- **Positive End-Expiratory Pressure (PEEP):** Apply PEEP to prevent atelectasis and improve oxygenation. The optimal level of PEEP varies based on individual patient characteristics and intraoperative conditions.
- **FiO2 Management:** Adjust the fraction of inspired oxygen (FiO2) to maintain oxygen saturation above 92-94%. Prolonged use of high FiO2 levels can lead to oxygen toxicity and absorption atelectasis, so titrate to the lowest effective concentration.

Monitoring and Adjustments

Continuous monitoring of respiratory parameters is essential for timely detection and correction of issues:

- **Capnography:** Measures end-tidal CO2 (EtCO2) levels, providing information about ventilation adequacy and helping detect hypo- or hyperventilation, equipment malfunctions, and changes in cardiac output.
- **Pulse Oximetry:** Monitors oxygen saturation, ensuring adequate oxygen delivery to tissues. Sudden drops in saturation can indicate issues such as airway obstruction, dislodgement of the endotracheal tube, or reduced cardiac output.
- **Arterial Blood Gas (ABG) Analysis**: Periodic ABG analysis is useful for assessing gas exchange, acid-base status, and guiding ventilatory adjustments.
- **Lung Mechanics:** Monitor parameters such as peak inspiratory pressure (PIP) and plateau pressure (Pplat) to avoid barotrauma and optimize ventilation settings.

Managing Intraoperative Respiratory Complications

Intraoperative respiratory complications can arise despite meticulous planning and management. Common issues include:

- **Bronchospasm:** Characterized by wheezing, increased airway resistance, and difficulty ventilating. Management includes deepening anesthesia, administering bronchodilators, and, if necessary, intravenous steroids.
- **Aspiration:** A serious complication that can lead to pneumonia and acute respiratory distress syndrome (ARDS). Preventive measures include fasting guidelines, the use of rapid-sequence induction, and cricoid pressure. Immediate management involves suctioning the airway, bronchoscopy, and supportive care.
- **Pneumothorax:** Can occur due to barotrauma or surgical injury. Symptoms include sudden desaturation, hypotension, and absence of breath sounds on the affected side. Management requires immediate decompression with a needle or chest tube placement.

Case Study: Managing Respiratory Care in a High-Risk Patient

Consider the case of a 65-year-old patient with severe COPD undergoing elective abdominal surgery. Preoperative optimization included bronchodilator therapy, corticosteroids, and intensive pulmonary rehabilitation. During surgery, a balanced anesthesia technique with a combination of regional and general anesthesia minimized respiratory depression. The patient was ventilated with low tidal volumes and moderate PEEP. Continuous monitoring allowed early detection and management of a bronchospasm episode, ensuring a smooth intraoperative course.

Intraoperative respiratory management is a dynamic and complex aspect of surgical care. By understanding the effects of anesthesia, employing appropriate mechanical ventilation strategies, and maintaining vigilant monitoring, healthcare providers can effectively manage respiratory function and mitigate complications.

DISCUSSION QUESTIONS

- How do different anesthesia techniques impact intraoperative respiratory management, and what are the pros and cons of each?
- What are the key considerations for monitoring and managing respiratory function during surgery to prevent intraoperative complications?

LESSON TWO: POSTOPERATIVE RESPIRATORY CARE AND MONITORING

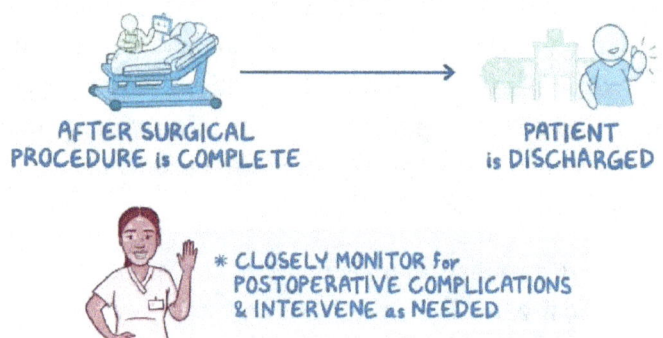

The postoperative period is a critical phase in respiratory care, where vigilant monitoring and proactive management are essential to ensure patient safety and promote recovery. Respiratory complications are common in the postoperative setting, necessitating a comprehensive approach to monitoring and intervention. This lesson outlines the principles and practices of postoperative respiratory care, emphasizing strategies to optimize outcomes and prevent complications.

Immediate Postoperative Care

Upon completion of surgery, patients are transferred to the post-anesthesia care unit (PACU) for close monitoring. Key components of immediate postoperative respiratory care include:

- **Airway Management:** Ensure the patency of the airway. Patients emerging from general anesthesia may have residual neuromuscular blockade or diminished reflexes, increasing the risk of airway obstruction. Techniques include positioning, suctioning, and, if necessary, placement of airway adjuncts such as oropharyngeal or nasopharyngeal airways.

- **Oxygen Therapy:** Administer supplemental oxygen to maintain adequate oxygen saturation. The method of delivery (nasal cannula, face mask, or high-flow oxygen) depends on the patient's needs and level of respiratory support required.
- **Monitoring**: Continuous monitoring of vital signs, oxygen saturation, and respiratory rate is essential. Early detection of hypoxemia, hypercapnia, or respiratory distress allows for timely intervention.

Pain Management and Its Impact on Respiratory Function

Effective pain management is crucial for optimizing respiratory function postoperatively. Pain, especially from thoracic or upper abdominal surgeries, can inhibit deep breathing and coughing, leading to atelectasis and pneumonia. Strategies for pain management include:

- **Multimodal Analgesia:** Combining different classes of analgesics (e.g., opioids, nonsteroidal anti-inflammatory drugs (NSAIDs), and local anesthetics) can enhance pain control while minimizing side effects.
- **Regional Anesthesia:** Techniques such as epidural analgesia or nerve blocks provide effective pain relief with minimal respiratory depression compared to systemic opioids.
- **Patient-Controlled Analgesia (PCA):** Allows patients to self-administer controlled doses of pain medication, providing effective pain relief while reducing the risk of overdose.

Respiratory Exercises and Physiotherapy

Encouraging patients to engage in respiratory exercises and physiotherapy is essential for preventing complications and promoting recovery:

- **Incentive Spirometry:** Instruct patients to use an incentive spirometer regularly to promote lung expansion and prevent atelectasis.

- **Deep Breathing Exercises:** Teach patients diaphragmatic breathing techniques to improve ventilation and oxygenation.
- **Chest Physiotherapy:** Techniques such as percussion, vibration, and postural drainage can help clear secretions and improve lung function.

Monitoring and Managing Respiratory Complications

Postoperative patients are at risk for several respiratory complications that require vigilant monitoring and prompt management:

- **Atelectasis:** Collapse of alveoli is common after surgery, particularly in patients who do not take deep breaths or cough effectively. Management includes incentive spirometry, deep breathing exercises, and early mobilization.
- **Pneumonia:** Hospital-acquired pneumonia is a significant risk, particularly in patients with prolonged intubation or immobility. Preventive measures include regular oral hygiene, maintaining adequate hydration, and using respiratory exercises.
- **Pulmonary Embolism (PE):** A potentially life-threatening condition where a blood clot travels to the lungs. Symptoms include sudden onset of dyspnea, chest pain, and hypoxemia. Management involves anticoagulation therapy and supportive care.
- **Acute Respiratory Distress Syndrome (ARDS):** A severe inflammatory response leading to respiratory failure. Management includes supportive care with mechanical ventilation using low tidal volumes, prone positioning, and addressing the underlying cause.

Special Considerations for High-Risk Patients

Certain populations require additional considerations and tailored approaches to postoperative respiratory care:

- **Elderly Patients:** Older adults are at increased risk of respiratory complications due to age-related changes in lung

function and comorbidities. A gentle approach to pain management, early mobilization, and close monitoring are crucial.
- **Patients with Obesity:** Obesity can impair respiratory mechanics and increase the risk of hypoventilation and obstructive sleep apnea (OSA). Postoperative care includes appropriate positioning, use of continuous positive airway pressure (CPAP) for OSA, and early ambulation.
- **Patients with Chronic Respiratory Conditions:** Those with preexisting conditions such as COPD or asthma require optimization of their baseline therapy and close monitoring for exacerbations. Tailored respiratory support and frequent reassessment are essential.

Case Study: Postoperative Care for a Patient with Obstructive Sleep Apnea

Consider a 55-year-old male with a history of obstructive sleep apnea (OSA) undergoing laparoscopic cholecystectomy. Postoperative care included:

- **CPAP Therapy:** Continuation of CPAP therapy during the postoperative period to prevent apneic episodes.
- **Pain Management:** Use of multimodal analgesia, including NSAIDs and local anesthetics, to minimize opioid use and reduce the risk of respiratory depression.
- **Monitoring:** Continuous pulse oximetry and capnography to detect early signs of hypoventilation and apnea.
- **Early Mobilization:** Encouragement to sit up and walk within hours of surgery to promote lung expansion and reduce the risk of complications.

DISCUSSION QUESTIONS

- What are the most common postoperative respiratory complications, and what strategies can be employed to prevent them?

- How does early mobilization and physiotherapy contribute to improved respiratory outcomes in postoperative patients?

MODULE THREE

LESSON ONE: COMMON RESPIRATORY COMPLICATIONS IN SURGERY AND THEIR MANAGEMENT

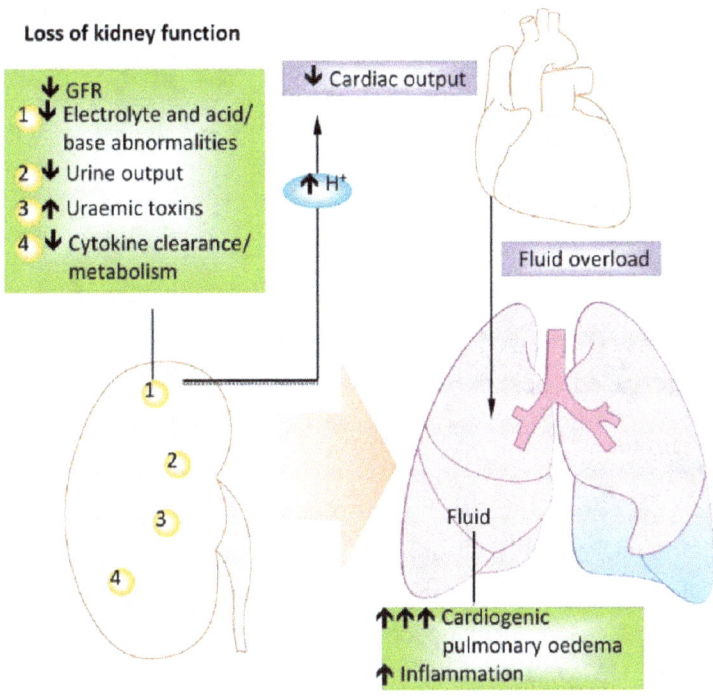

Lung injury and oedema

Respiratory complications are among the most common and potentially severe issues encountered in surgical patients. Recognizing, preventing, and managing these complications is essential for ensuring patient safety and promoting recovery. This lesson provides an in-depth look at common respiratory complications in surgery, including their etiology, clinical presentation, and management strategies.

1. ATELECTASIS

Atelectasis, the collapse of part or all of a lung, is a frequent postoperative complication, particularly following thoracic and upper abdominal surgeries.

Etiology and Risk Factors

- Hypoventilation: Due to pain, anesthesia, and immobility.
- Obstruction: Mucus plugs or foreign bodies blocking the airways.
- Compression: External pressure from pleural effusion or tumors.

Clinical Presentation

- Symptoms: Dyspnea, cough, and pleuritic chest pain.
- Signs: Decreased breath sounds, dullness on percussion, and decreased chest expansion.

Management

- Prevention: Incentive spirometry, deep breathing exercises, and early mobilization.
- Treatment: Chest physiotherapy, bronchodilators, and in severe cases, bronchoscopy to remove obstructions.

2. PNEUMONIA

Postoperative pneumonia is a significant cause of morbidity and mortality, particularly in patients with prolonged mechanical ventilation or impaired immune systems.

Etiology and Risk Factors

- Aspiration: Inhalation of oropharyngeal or gastric contents.
- Infection: Bacterial, viral, or fungal pathogens.

Clinical Presentation

- Symptoms: Fever, productive cough, dyspnea, and chest pain.

- Signs: Crackles on auscultation, increased respiratory rate, and hypoxemia.

Management

- Prevention: Elevate the head of the bed, maintain oral hygiene, and ensure adequate hydration.
- Treatment: Empirical antibiotics based on local resistance patterns, supportive care with oxygen therapy, and physiotherapy.

3. PULMONARY EMBOLISM (PE)

Pulmonary embolism, the blockage of a pulmonary artery by a thrombus, is a life-threatening condition that requires prompt diagnosis and treatment.

Etiology and Risk Factors

- Deep Vein Thrombosis (DVT): Thrombi originating from the lower extremities.
- Hypercoagulable States: Surgery, cancer, and immobility.

Clinical Presentation

- Symptoms: Sudden onset of dyspnea, chest pain, and hemoptysis.
- Signs: Tachycardia, hypotension, and decreased oxygen saturation.

Management

- Prevention: Prophylactic anticoagulation, mechanical prophylaxis (e.g., compression stockings), and early ambulation.
- Treatment: Anticoagulation therapy (heparin, warfarin, or direct oral anticoagulants), thrombolytic therapy for massive PE, and supportive care with oxygen and fluids.

4. ACUTE RESPIRATORY DISTRESS SYNDROME (ARDS)

ARDS is a severe inflammatory response that leads to acute respiratory failure and requires intensive care management.

Etiology and Risk Factors

- Sepsis: Systemic infection leading to widespread inflammation.
- Trauma: Severe injury or surgery causing lung damage.

Clinical Presentation

- Symptoms: Rapid onset of severe dyspnea, tachypnea, and hypoxemia.
- Signs: Bilateral infiltrates on chest imaging, decreased lung compliance, and refractory hypoxemia.

Management

- Supportive Care: Mechanical ventilation with lung-protective strategies (low tidal volumes and PEEP).
- Treatment of Underlying Cause: Addressing sepsis, trauma, or other triggers.
- Adjunctive Therapies: Prone positioning, extracorporeal membrane oxygenation (ECMO) in severe cases.

Case Study: Managing Postoperative Pneumonia

Consider a 70-year-old female with a history of diabetes and hypertension undergoing hip replacement surgery. Postoperatively, she developed fever, productive cough, and hypoxemia. Management included:

- Early Diagnosis: Chest X-ray confirmed pneumonia, and sputum culture identified the causative organism.
- Antibiotic Therapy: Initiation of broad-spectrum antibiotics tailored to culture results.

- Supportive Care: Supplemental oxygen, incentive spirometry, and hydration to aid recovery.

DISCUSSION QUESTIONS

- How do different respiratory therapies (e.g., mechanical ventilation, non-invasive ventilation) vary in their application and effectiveness for surgical patients?
- What are the key factors to consider when selecting and implementing respiratory interventions in postoperative care?

LESSON TWO: RESPIRATORY THERAPIES AND INTERVENTIONS IN SURGICAL PATIENTS

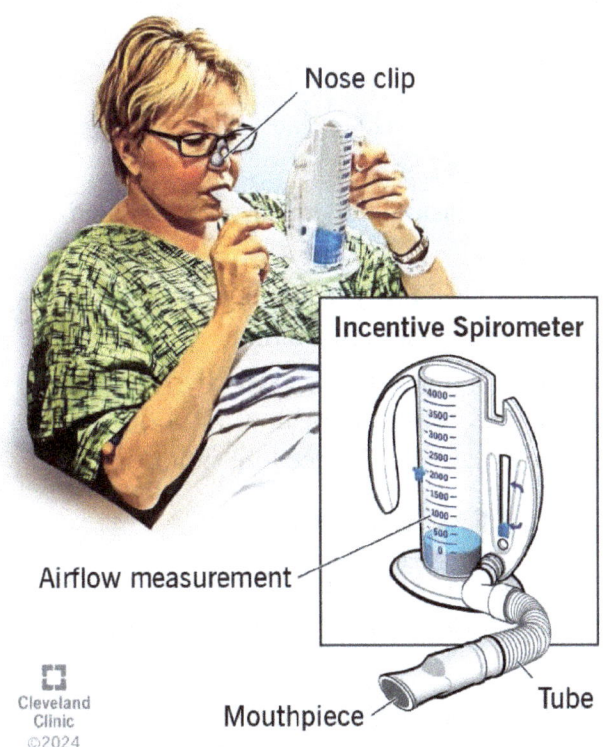

Respiratory therapies and interventions play a pivotal role in the perioperative management of surgical patients. These therapies aim to optimize respiratory function, prevent complications, and support recovery. This lesson provides an overview of various respiratory therapies and interventions, detailing their indications, techniques, and expected outcomes.

OXYGEN THERAPY

Oxygen therapy is a fundamental component of respiratory care, essential for maintaining adequate oxygenation in surgical patients.

Indications

- Hypoxemia: Low blood oxygen levels due to anesthesia, surgery, or underlying conditions.
- Respiratory Distress: Conditions such as pneumonia, PE, or ARDS.

Delivery Methods

- Nasal Cannula: Provides low to moderate concentrations of oxygen (up to 6 L/min).
- Simple Face Mask: Delivers moderate oxygen concentrations (6-10 L/min).
- Non-Rebreather Mask: Offers high concentrations of oxygen (10-15 L/min) without rebreathing exhaled air.
- High-Flow Nasal Cannula (HFNC): Delivers heated and humidified oxygen at high flow rates, providing respiratory support and reducing the need for intubation.

MECHANICAL VENTILATION

Mechanical ventilation is a critical intervention for patients who cannot maintain adequate ventilation and oxygenation on their own.

Indications

- Respiratory Failure: Due to ARDS, severe pneumonia, or exacerbation of chronic respiratory conditions.

- Intraoperative Support: For patients undergoing major surgeries with general anesthesia.

Modes and Settings

- Volume-Controlled Ventilation (VCV): Delivers a set tidal volume with each breath.
- Pressure-Controlled Ventilation (PCV): Delivers breaths at a set pressure, with tidal volume varying.
- Positive End-Expiratory Pressure (PEEP): Prevents alveolar collapse by maintaining positive pressure at the end of expiration.
- Weaning Protocols: Gradually reduce ventilatory support to assess the patient's ability to breathe independently. Techniques include spontaneous breathing trials (SBTs) and gradual reduction of pressure support.
- Extubation Criteria: Ensure the patient is alert, has stable vital signs, adequate oxygenation, and minimal secretions before removing the endotracheal tube.

NON-INVASIVE VENTILATION (NIV)

NIV provides ventilatory support without the need for intubation, using interfaces such as masks or nasal devices.

Indications

- Respiratory Failure: Particularly effective for patients with COPD exacerbations, cardiogenic pulmonary edema, and OSA.
- Postoperative Respiratory Support: To prevent reintubation in patients who struggle with weaning from mechanical ventilation.

Techniques

- Continuous Positive Airway Pressure (CPAP): Maintains a continuous level of positive pressure throughout the respiratory cycle to keep airways open.

- Bi-Level Positive Airway Pressure (BiPAP): Provides two levels of pressure – higher during inhalation and lower during exhalation – to support breathing efforts.

AIRWAY CLEARANCE TECHNIQUES

Effective clearance of secretions is crucial for preventing respiratory complications and optimizing lung function.

Indications

- Retained Secretions: In patients with conditions such as cystic fibrosis, bronchiectasis, or after surgery.
- Atelectasis: To promote re-expansion of collapsed alveoli.

Techniques

- Chest Physiotherapy (CPT): Includes postural drainage, percussion, and vibration to loosen and mobilize secretions.
- Mechanical Devices: High-frequency chest wall oscillation (HFCWO) vests and positive expiratory pressure (PEP) devices aid in secretion clearance.
- Cough Assist Devices: Provide mechanical assistance to enhance cough effectiveness, particularly in patients with neuromuscular weakness.

INHALATION THERAPY

Administering medications directly into the respiratory tract can provide targeted treatment and improve outcomes.

Indications

- Bronchodilation: For patients with bronchospasm, such as those with asthma or COPD.
- Anti-Inflammatory: To reduce airway inflammation and prevent exacerbations.

Techniques

- Metered-Dose Inhalers (MDIs): Deliver precise doses of medication, often used with spacers to enhance delivery.
- Nebulizers: Convert liquid medications into aerosol form for inhalation, useful for patients who have difficulty with MDIs.
- Dry Powder Inhalers (DPIs): Provide powdered medication that is inhaled deeply into the lungs.

ADVANCED RESPIRATORY SUPPORT

For critically ill patients, advanced respiratory support techniques may be required.

Indications

- Severe Respiratory Failure: Where conventional mechanical ventilation is insufficient.
- Refractory Hypoxemia: In conditions like ARDS.

Techniques

- Extracorporeal Membrane Oxygenation (ECMO): Provides prolonged cardiac and respiratory support by circulating blood through an artificial lung.
- Prone Positioning: Enhances oxygenation by improving ventilation-perfusion matching in patients with ARDS.

Case Study: Non-Invasive Ventilation in Postoperative Care

Consider a 60-year-old female with a history of COPD undergoing major abdominal surgery. Postoperatively, she developed respiratory distress and hypercapnia. Management included:

- Early NIV Initiation: BiPAP was started to support her breathing and improve gas exchange.
- Continuous Monitoring: Regular assessments of respiratory rate, oxygen saturation, and blood gases to guide therapy adjustments.

- Comprehensive Care: Including bronchodilator therapy, chest physiotherapy, and incentive spirometry to enhance lung function.

Respiratory therapies and interventions are integral to the care of surgical patients, playing a crucial role in optimizing respiratory function, preventing complications, and supporting recovery. By understanding the indications, techniques, and expected outcomes of these therapies, healthcare providers can deliver effective and tailored respiratory care.

DISCUSSION QUESTIONS

- What are the indications for advanced respiratory support techniques like ECMO, and how do they improve outcomes in critically ill surgical patients?
- How do healthcare providers determine when to transition from conventional respiratory support to more advanced methods?

MODULE FOUR

LESSON ONE: THE ROLE OF MULTIDISCIPLINARY TEAMS IN RESPIRATORY CARE

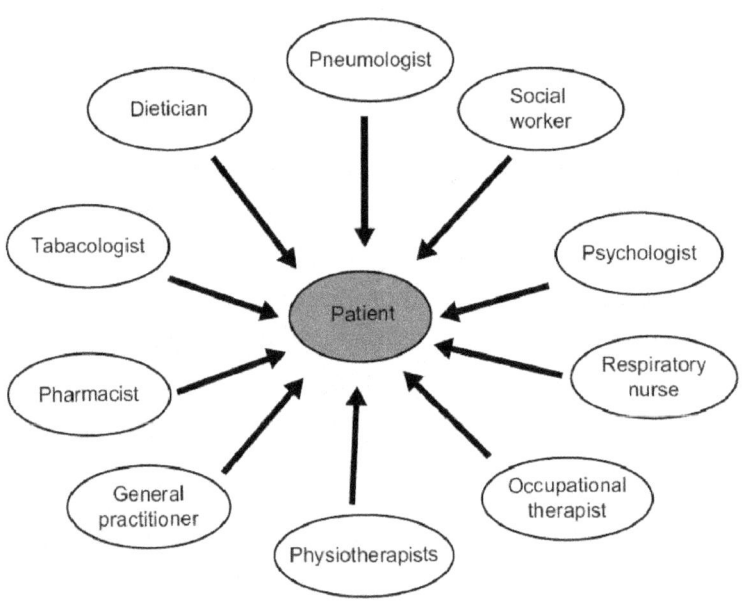

Effective respiratory care in surgical patients requires a collaborative approach involving multidisciplinary teams. These teams bring together diverse expertise to address the complex needs of patients, ensuring comprehensive and coordinated care. This lesson explores the roles and contributions of various healthcare professionals in respiratory care, highlighting the importance of teamwork and communication.

The Multidisciplinary Team

A multidisciplinary team for respiratory care typically includes:

- Surgeons: Responsible for the surgical procedure and postoperative care, they play a critical role in planning and coordinating respiratory management.

- Anesthesiologists: Experts in perioperative medicine, they manage anesthesia, airway control, and intraoperative ventilation, and contribute to postoperative respiratory care.
- Respiratory Therapists: Specialize in assessing and managing respiratory function, providing therapies such as mechanical ventilation, oxygen therapy, and airway clearance.
- Nurses: Integral to patient care, they monitor respiratory status, administer medications, provide patient education, and support early mobilization.
- Physiotherapists: Focus on respiratory exercises, chest physiotherapy, and early mobilization to improve lung function and prevent complications.
- Pharmacists: Ensure appropriate medication management, including pain relief, bronchodilators, and antibiotics, and provide drug interaction assessments.
- Pulmonologists: Provide specialized care for patients with complex respiratory conditions, offering expertise in diagnosis and management.
- Dietitians: Address nutritional needs to support recovery and optimize respiratory function, particularly in patients with chronic respiratory conditions.

COLLABORATION AND COMMUNICATION

Effective collaboration and communication among team members are essential for delivering high-quality respiratory care.

Interdisciplinary Rounds

- Daily Meetings: Regular interdisciplinary rounds allow team members to discuss patient progress, identify issues, and develop coordinated care plans.
- Shared Decision-Making: Involving all team members in decision-making ensures that diverse perspectives are considered, leading to more comprehensive care plans.

Communication Tools

- Electronic Health Records (EHRs): Facilitate information sharing and coordination of care across disciplines.
- Handover Protocols: Structured handover protocols ensure that critical information is communicated during transitions of care, such as shift changes or transfers between units.

EDUCATION AND TRAINING

Continuous education and training are vital for maintaining high standards of respiratory care.

Professional Development

- Workshops and Seminars: Regular training sessions on the latest respiratory care techniques and technologies keep team members updated.
- Simulation Training: Simulated scenarios allow team members to practice managing respiratory emergencies and refine their skills in a safe environment.

Patient and Family Education

- Preoperative Counseling: Educating patients and families about the importance of respiratory care, expected outcomes, and postoperative exercises.
- Discharge Planning: Providing clear instructions and resources for continuing respiratory care at home, including the use of respiratory devices and exercises.

QUALITY IMPROVEMENT AND RESEARCH

Engaging in quality improvement initiatives and research is essential for advancing respiratory care practices.

Quality Improvement Projects

- Audits and Feedback: Regular audits of respiratory care practices, followed by feedback sessions to identify areas for improvement and implement changes.
- Clinical Pathways: Developing and refining clinical pathways for respiratory care to standardize practices and enhance outcomes.

Research and Innovation

- Clinical Trials: Participating in clinical trials to evaluate new therapies and interventions in respiratory care.
- Evidence-Based Practice: Implementing evidence-based guidelines and protocols to ensure the highest standards of care.

Case Study: Multidisciplinary Care for a Complex Respiratory Patient

Consider a 72-year-old male with severe COPD and a history of congestive heart failure undergoing coronary artery bypass grafting (CABG). The multidisciplinary team approach included:

- Preoperative Optimization: Collaboration between pulmonologists and cardiologists to optimize the patient's respiratory and cardiac status before surgery.
- Intraoperative Management: Anesthesiologists ensured optimal ventilation strategies and close monitoring during surgery.
- Postoperative Care: Respiratory therapists provided non-invasive ventilation and chest physiotherapy, while nurses monitored respiratory status and managed pain.
- Follow-Up and Discharge Planning: Dietitians and physiotherapists developed a comprehensive discharge plan, including nutritional support and home-based respiratory exercises.

DISCUSSION QUESTIONS

- How does interdisciplinary collaboration enhance respiratory care in surgical patients, and what are the key roles of different team members?
- What are the challenges and benefits of implementing a multidisciplinary approach to respiratory care in a surgical setting?

LESSON TWO: FUTURE TRENDS IN RESPIRATORY CARE

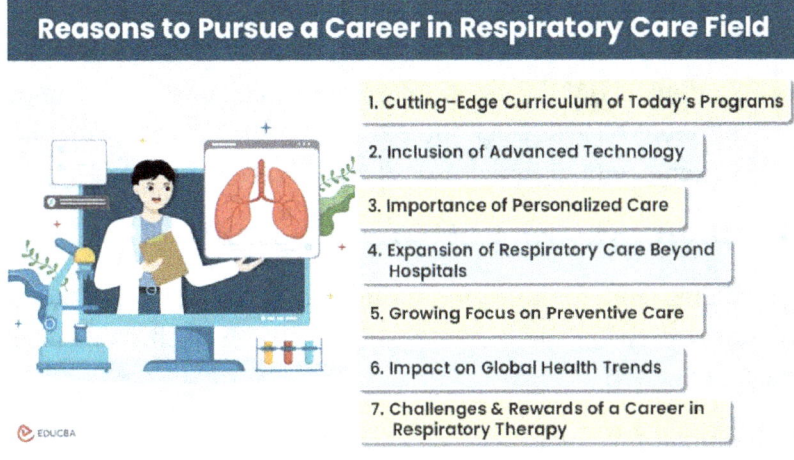

The field of respiratory care is continually evolving, driven by advances in technology, research, and clinical practice. Emerging trends and innovations hold the promise of improving patient outcomes and transforming respiratory care. This lesson explores the future directions in respiratory care, highlighting key technologies and practices that are set to shape the field.

ADVANCES IN MECHANICAL VENTILATION

Innovations in mechanical ventilation technology are enhancing the ability to support patients with respiratory failure more effectively.

Smart Ventilators

- Adaptive Support Ventilation (ASV): Automatically adjusts ventilation parameters based on patient needs, optimizing support and reducing the risk of ventilator-induced lung injury.
- Closed-Loop Systems: Use real-time data to continuously adjust ventilatory support, ensuring precise and responsive care.

Non-Invasive Ventilation (NIV) Enhancements

- Improved Interfaces: Development of more comfortable and effective masks and nasal devices to enhance patient compliance.
- Portable NIV Devices: Increasing availability of compact, portable NIV devices for use outside the hospital, supporting patients with chronic respiratory conditions.

TELEMEDICINE AND REMOTE MONITORING

Telemedicine and remote monitoring are revolutionizing the way respiratory care is delivered, particularly for chronic disease management.

Tele-Respiratory Care

- Virtual Consultations: Enable patients to receive expert respiratory care without the need to travel, improving access and convenience.
- Remote Monitoring: Use of wearable devices and home monitoring systems to track respiratory parameters, allowing for early intervention and continuous care.

Data Analytics and Artificial Intelligence (AI)

- Predictive Analytics: AI-driven algorithms can analyze patient data to predict respiratory complications and guide proactive interventions.

- Personalized Care Plans: Using data analytics to tailor respiratory care plans to individual patient needs, optimizing outcomes.

NOVEL THERAPEUTIC APPROACHES

Research is uncovering new therapeutic approaches that have the potential to transform respiratory care.

Regenerative Medicine

- Stem Cell Therapy: Investigating the use of stem cells to repair and regenerate damaged lung tissue, offering hope for conditions like COPD and pulmonary fibrosis.
- Gene Therapy: Exploring the potential of gene editing techniques to correct genetic defects underlying respiratory diseases.

Innovative Drug Delivery Systems

- Nanotechnology: Development of nanoparticle-based drug delivery systems to enhance the efficacy and targeting of respiratory medications.
- Smart Inhalers: Devices that track medication usage and provide feedback to ensure adherence and optimize treatment.

ENHANCING PATIENT ENGAGEMENT AND EDUCATION

Empowering patients through education and engagement is crucial for the success of respiratory care.

Digital Health Tools

- Mobile Apps: Apps designed to educate patients, track symptoms, and provide reminders for medication and respiratory exercises.
- Virtual Reality (VR): Using VR for patient education and training, offering immersive experiences to teach respiratory techniques and exercises.

Community and Peer Support

- Online Support Groups: Facilitating connections between patients with similar conditions, providing emotional support and shared experiences.
- Patient Advocacy: Encouraging patients to take an active role in their care, advocating for their needs and preferences.

Case Study: Telemedicine in Managing Chronic Respiratory Disease

Consider a 65-year-old male with advanced COPD living in a rural area with limited access to specialist care. Telemedicine allowed for:

- Regular Virtual Consultations: Monthly check-ins with a pulmonologist to manage his condition and adjust treatment as needed.
- Remote Monitoring: Use of a home spirometer and pulse oximeter to track his respiratory status, with data transmitted to his healthcare team for continuous monitoring.
- Education and Support: Access to online resources and support groups, enhancing his understanding of the condition and connecting him with others facing similar challenges.

DISCUSSION QUESTIONS

- How might emerging technologies like smart ventilators and telemedicine transform the landscape of respiratory care in surgery?
- What are the potential ethical and practical implications of integrating AI and remote monitoring into respiratory care practices?

MODULE FIVE

LESSON ONE: ETHICAL CONSIDERATIONS IN RESPIRATORY CARE

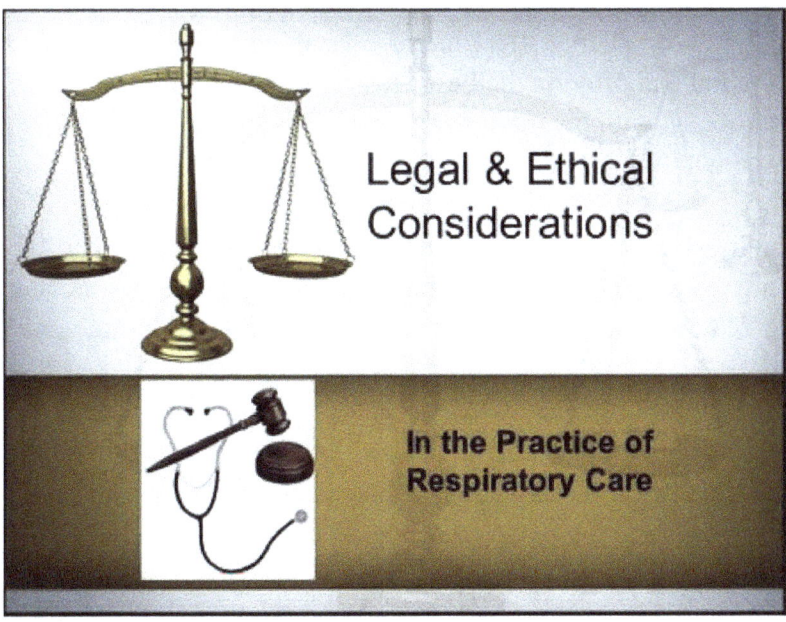

Ethical considerations are integral to the practice of respiratory care, particularly in the surgical setting. Healthcare providers frequently face complex ethical dilemmas that require balancing patient autonomy, beneficence, non-maleficence, and justice. This lesson explores key ethical principles, common ethical challenges, and strategies for navigating these issues in respiratory care.

KEY ETHICAL PRINCIPLES

Autonomy

- Respect for Patient Autonomy: Ensuring that patients have the right to make informed decisions about their care. This includes providing comprehensive information about treatment options, risks, and benefits.

- Informed Consent: Obtaining informed consent is crucial, particularly for procedures like mechanical ventilation or surgery. Patients should understand the implications and potential outcomes.

Beneficence

Acting in the Patient's Best Interest: Healthcare providers must aim to do good and provide the best possible care, balancing the benefits of treatments with potential harms.

Non-Maleficence

Avoiding Harm: This principle emphasizes the importance of not causing harm to patients. In respiratory care, this includes preventing complications and minimizing the risks associated with interventions.

Justice

Fairness and Equity: Ensuring fair distribution of healthcare resources and equal access to care. This is particularly relevant in managing scarce resources like ICU beds or ventilators during pandemics.

COMMON ETHICAL CHALLENGES

End-of-Life Decisions

- Withdrawal of Life Support: Deciding when to withdraw mechanical ventilation can be challenging, requiring careful consideration of the patient's prognosis, quality of life, and wishes.
- Advance Directives: Respecting advance directives and living wills, which outline patients' preferences for end-of-life care.

Allocation of Resources

- Scarcity of Resources: During crises such as pandemics, ethical dilemmas arise over the allocation of limited resources like ventilators. Ethical frameworks guide these decisions to ensure fairness and transparency.

- Triage Protocols: Implementing triage protocols based on clinical criteria to prioritize care for patients most likely to benefit.

Confidentiality and Privacy

- Protecting Patient Information: Ensuring that patient confidentiality is maintained, particularly when using telemedicine and electronic health records.
- Data Security: Safeguarding sensitive patient data from unauthorized access and breaches.

STRATEGIES FOR ETHICAL DECISION-MAKING

Ethical Frameworks

- Principle-Based Approach: Applying the four key ethical principles (autonomy, beneficence, non-maleficence, and justice) to guide decision-making.
- Case-Based Approach: Analyzing specific cases to draw parallels with past decisions, ensuring consistency and fairness.

Ethical Committees

- Multidisciplinary Ethics Committees: These committees provide a forum for discussing complex ethical issues, offering diverse perspectives and expertise to support decision-making.
- Ethics Consultations: Seeking advice from ethics consultants or committees for particularly challenging cases.

Communication and Collaboration

- Open Communication: Maintaining open and honest communication with patients and families, involving them in decision-making processes.

- Interdisciplinary Collaboration: Working closely with other healthcare professionals to ensure a holistic approach to patient care, particularly when ethical dilemmas arise.

Case Study: Ethical Dilemma in Respiratory Care

Consider a 68-year-old patient with advanced COPD admitted for elective surgery. Postoperatively, the patient develops severe respiratory failure requiring prolonged mechanical ventilation. The patient's advance directive indicates a preference against long-term life support, but the family insists on continuing aggressive treatment. The healthcare team faces the ethical dilemma of respecting the patient's wishes versus the family's desires. An ethics consultation is sought to facilitate discussion and reach a consensus.

Ethical considerations are a fundamental aspect of respiratory care, requiring healthcare providers to navigate complex dilemmas with sensitivity and professionalism. By applying ethical principles, seeking guidance from ethics committees, and fostering open communication, providers can ensure that care is delivered with respect, fairness, and compassion.

DISCUSSION QUESTIONS

- How can healthcare providers balance patient autonomy with the need for life-saving interventions in respiratory care?
- What strategies can be implemented to ensure fair allocation of resources like ventilators during a healthcare crisis?

MODULE SIX

LESSON ONE: CULTURAL COMPETENCE IN RESPIRATORY CARE

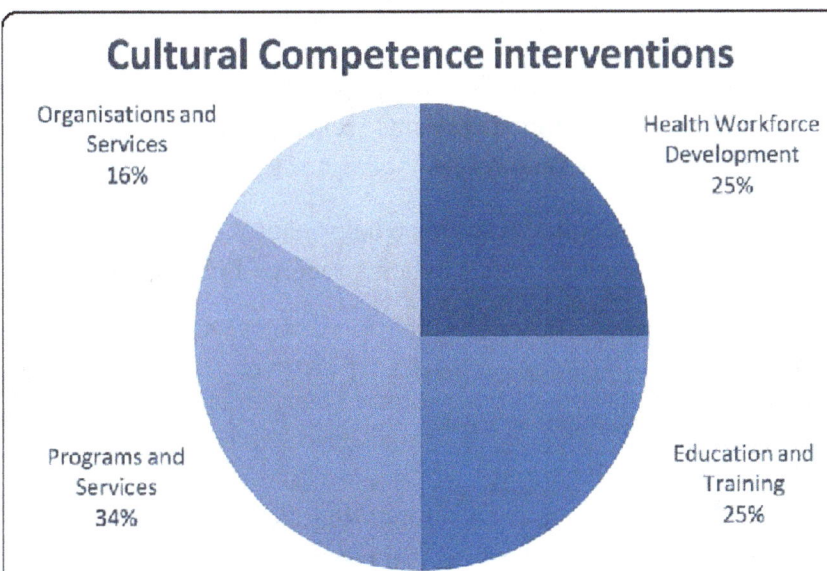

Cultural competence is essential in providing effective respiratory care, particularly in a diverse, multicultural society. Understanding and respecting cultural differences can significantly impact patient outcomes and satisfaction. This lesson explores the importance of cultural competence, strategies for developing cultural awareness, and practical approaches for delivering culturally sensitive respiratory care.

THE IMPORTANCE OF CULTURAL COMPETENCE

1. **Enhancing Patient Communication**
   - Effective Communication: Understanding cultural nuances improves communication with patients and their families, fostering trust and ensuring that information is accurately conveyed.

- Language Barriers: Addressing language barriers through translation services and bilingual staff helps ensure that patients fully understand their care and treatment options.

2. **Improving Patient Outcomes**
   - Tailored Care: Providing care that respects cultural beliefs and practices can enhance adherence to treatment plans and improve health outcomes.
   - Patient Satisfaction: Culturally competent care leads to higher patient satisfaction, as patients feel respected and understood.

3. **Reducing Health Disparities**

Equitable Care: Cultural competence helps address and reduce health disparities by ensuring that all patients receive fair and appropriate care, regardless of their background.

STRATEGIES FOR DEVELOPING CULTURAL COMPETENCE

1. **Education and Training**
   - Cultural Competency Training: Regular training programs for healthcare providers to increase awareness of cultural differences and develop skills for providing culturally sensitive care.
   - Continuing Education: Encouraging ongoing learning about cultural issues and their impact on health care through workshops, seminars, and courses.

2. **Self-Reflection**
   - Personal Biases: Encouraging healthcare providers to reflect on their own biases and assumptions, and how these may impact patient care.
   - Cultural Humility: Adopting an attitude of cultural humility, recognizing the limitations of one's own cultural perspective and being open to learning from patients.

3. **Institutional Support**
   - Policies and Protocols: Implementing policies that promote cultural competence within healthcare institutions, such as guidelines for using interpreters and cultural liaison officers.

- Diverse Workforce: Promoting diversity within the healthcare workforce to reflect the community served and enhance cultural understanding.

PRACTICAL APPROACHES FOR CULTURALLY SENSITIVE CARE

1. Communication Techniques
- Language Services: Providing professional medical interpreters and translation services to ensure clear and accurate communication.
- Cultural Brokers: Utilizing cultural brokers who can bridge cultural gaps and facilitate understanding between patients and providers.

2. Culturally Adapted Care Plans
- Respecting Beliefs: Incorporating patients' cultural beliefs and practices into care plans, such as dietary restrictions, traditional healing practices, and preferences for end-of-life care.
- Family Involvement: Recognizing the role of family in decision-making processes and involving them in care discussions when appropriate.

Case Study: Culturally Competent Respiratory Care

Consider a 45-year-old patient from a Middle Eastern background admitted for lung surgery. The patient and family have specific cultural and religious beliefs regarding illness and treatment. The healthcare team:

- Engages an Interpreter: To ensure clear communication about the surgery and postoperative care.
- Incorporates Cultural Beliefs: By accommodating the patient's prayer schedule and dietary needs.
- Involves the Family: In discussions about care plans and respects their input and cultural practices.

DISCUSSION QUESTIONS

- How does cultural competence impact patient outcomes in respiratory care, and what are effective strategies for developing cultural awareness among healthcare providers?
- What are the challenges of providing culturally sensitive respiratory care, and how can these be addressed within a healthcare team?

MODULE SEVEN

LESSON ONE: PSYCHOLOGICAL ASPECTS OF RESPIRATORY CARE

The psychological well-being of patients significantly influences respiratory health and recovery, particularly in the context of surgery. Anxiety,

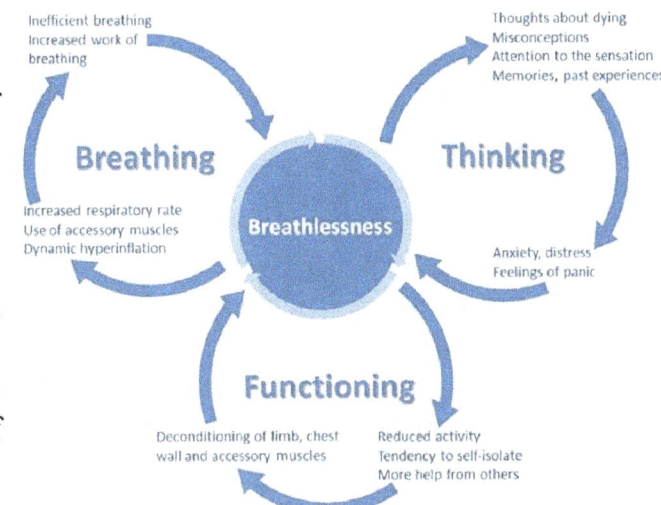

depression, and stress can adversely affect respiratory function and complicate postoperative care. This lesson examines the psychological aspects of respiratory care, the impact of mental health on respiratory outcomes, and strategies for integrating psychological support into patient care.

THE IMPACT OF MENTAL HEALTH ON RESPIRATORY FUNCTION

1. **Anxiety and Stress**
   - Respiratory Effects: Anxiety and stress can lead to hyperventilation, increased respiratory rate, and bronchoconstriction, exacerbating respiratory conditions.
   - Preoperative Anxiety: High levels of preoperative anxiety can impair recovery and increase the risk of postoperative complications.

2. **Depression**
   - Impact on Recovery: Depression is associated with poor adherence to treatment, reduced physical activity, and prolonged recovery times.
   - Physiological Effects: Chronic depression can lead to systemic inflammation, which may worsen respiratory conditions such as asthma and COPD.

PSYCHOLOGICAL ASSESSMENT IN RESPIRATORY CARE

Screening Tools

- Questionnaires and Scales: Utilizing standardized tools such as the Hospital Anxiety and Depression Scale (HADS) to assess patients' psychological well-being.
- Clinical Interviews: Conducting comprehensive assessments through clinical interviews to identify psychological issues that may impact respiratory health.

Integrating Psychological Care

- Multidisciplinary Approach: Collaborating with psychologists, psychiatrists, and counselors to provide holistic care that addresses both physical and mental health needs.
- Referral Systems: Establishing clear referral pathways for patients requiring specialized psychological support.

STRATEGIES FOR MANAGING PSYCHOLOGICAL DISTRESS

1. **Preoperative Counseling**
   - Education and Reassurance: Providing detailed information about the surgical procedure and expected outcomes to reduce anxiety.
   - Relaxation Techniques: Teaching relaxation techniques such as deep breathing exercises, progressive muscle relaxation, and mindfulness to manage anxiety.

2. **Postoperative Support**
   - Pain Management: Effective pain control to reduce anxiety and improve comfort during recovery.
   - Emotional Support: Offering emotional support through regular check-ins, counseling, and support groups to address feelings of depression and isolation.

Case Study: Managing Preoperative Anxiety

Consider a 50-year-old patient scheduled for lung surgery who exhibits high levels of preoperative anxiety. The healthcare team:

- Provides Preoperative Education: Detailed explanations of the procedure, recovery process, and potential complications to alleviate fears.
- Teaches Relaxation Techniques: Guided breathing exercises and mindfulness practices to help the patient manage anxiety.
- Involves a Counselor: Referral to a counselor for preoperative sessions to address underlying anxiety and develop coping strategies.

DISCUSSION QUESTIONS

- How do anxiety and depression affect respiratory function in surgical patients, and what interventions can be implemented to address these psychological issues?
- What role do preoperative counseling and postoperative emotional support play in improving respiratory outcomes, and how can these be effectively integrated into patient care?

CONCLUSION

Respiratory care in surgery is a multifaceted and critical component of patient management, spanning the entire surgical continuum from preoperative assessment to postoperative recovery. This comprehensive guide has delved into various aspects of respiratory care, emphasizing the importance of meticulous planning, advanced therapeutic interventions, and a holistic approach to patient well-being.

The fundamentals of respiratory care highlight the physiological intricacies that must be understood to optimize patient outcomes. Preoperative assessments are vital in identifying risks and tailoring interventions to individual patient needs. During surgery, careful intraoperative management is essential to maintain respiratory stability and prevent complications.

Respiratory care in surgery is a dynamic and evolving field that demands a thorough understanding of medical principles, a commitment to patient-centered care, and an openness to innovation. By adhering to best practices, embracing technological advancements, and fostering a culturally competent and ethically sound approach, healthcare providers can significantly enhance the quality of respiratory care. This, in turn, leads to better surgical outcomes, improved patient satisfaction, and a higher standard of healthcare delivery overall.

By equipping healthcare providers with the knowledge and tools outlined in this guide, we hope to empower them to deliver exceptional respiratory care and support to their patients, ultimately improving the health and well-being of those undergoing surgery.

REFERENCES

Chiumello, D., Brochard, L., Marini, J.J. (2017). *Respiratory Support in the Intensive Care Unit. American Journal of Respiratory and Critical Care Medicine.*

Fan, E., Brodie, D., Slutsky, A.S. (2018). *Acute Respiratory Distress Syndrome: Advances in Diagnosis and Treatment. JAMA.*

Flenady, V.J., MacDonald, A.M., Flenady, V., Wilson, A. (2017). *Ventilator Strategies for the Acute Respiratory Distress Syndrome. Cochrane Database of Systematic Reviews.*

Hess, D.R. (2015*). Respiratory Care: Principles and Practice. Jones & Bartlett Learning.*

Hill, N.S., Brennan, J., Garpestad, E., Nava, S. (2020*). Noninvasive Ventilation in Acute Respiratory Failure. Critical Care Medicine.*

Kallet, R.H., Dicker, R.A. (2019). *How to Write and Implement an Effective Respiratory Therapy Protocol Program. Respiratory Care.*

Koutsoukou, A., Armaganidis, A., Mouloudi, E., Georgopoulos, D. (2016). *Respiratory Physiotherapy in the Intensive Care Unit. Annals of Thoracic Medicine.*

MacIntyre, N.R., Branson, R.D. (2018). *Mechanical Ventilation: The Essentials. Elsevier.*

Maselli, D.J., Keyt, H., Restrepo, M.I. (2017). *Inhaled Antibiotics in Mechanically Ventilated Patients. Respiratory Care.*

Perkins, G.D., Mistry, D., Gates, S., Gao, F., Snelson, C. (2016). Effect of Protocolized Weaning with Early Extubation to Non-Invasive Ventilation. JAMA.

Pinsky, M.R., Brochard, L. (2019). Applied Physiology in Intensive Care Medicine. Springer.